NORTH AMERICAN
P-51
MUSTANG

by

Edward T. Maloney and Uwe Feist

Aero Publishers, Inc.

329 Aviation Road   Fallbrook, California

© **AERO PUBLISHERS, INC.**

1967

Library of Congress Catalog Card Number

67-21487

Printed and Published in the United States of America by Aero Publishers, Inc.

NORTH AMERICAN P-51 MUSTANG

By Edward T. Maloney
Curator, The Air Museum
Ontario, California

The American Mustang fighter of World War II was an aerial dark horse. It was built entirely from information garnered from the battlefield. Packed into its trim airframe were more radical ideas than any single airplane in the history of fighter aircraft. Yet it was blended so subtly that our own Air Force at first passed this ship off as just another untried aircraft.

In the spring of 1940, Great Britain was fighting for its life in the air war over Europe. A special British Purchasing Commission was sent to the United States to buy badly needed aircraft. One day the Commission conferred with "Dutch" Kindelberger who was president of a relatively new airplane company on the West Coast. The English representatives wanted Kindelberger to build the Curtiss P-40 "Kittyhawk" fighter under license. Kindelberger did not believe this aircraft was suitable for combat over Europe against the highly maneuverable German Messerschmitt Bf-109 fighter and he told the commission he preferred to design and build a new fighter—one that would incorporate all the lessons learned from the battlefield. The Commission protested, stating their need was now and not two years hence, the amount of time normally required for this task. Kindelberger gave a blunt reply, "Give me 120 days and you'll have your fighter!" The British Commission officials just smiled but left their forwarding address just in case their specifications for this 120-day miracle fighter came about.

Kindelberger headed West with his new contract. He assigned Edgar Schmued as chief design engineer; however, many engineers participated in the design.

The basic engineering problem was to design a fighter that would outperform its Axis rival in maneuverability and top speed. Wind tunnel tests showed that shock waves were the largest problem affecting speed. A new wing was designed incorporating the new laminar flow wing. The aircraft was to be powered by an Allison 12-cylinder, liquid-cooled Vee engine. It was also designed with a belly mounted ram intake. The trim fuselage lines were created in record time by a purely mathematical system known as development of secondary degree curves. This new system gave designers the best absolute system for determining the best streamlining between two given points.

The Royal Air Force designated this North American NA-73 design the Mustang I. The first airplane was completed in the fall of 1940 and was tested during the winter of 1940. Full production was immediately ordered in the spring of 1941. News of its advance performance attracted the Air Material Command of the Army Air Force and an order was issued to procure one for tests at Wright Field. The fifth production Mustang became the first of two XP-51 "Apache's". Little interest was shown at first by the Air Force, as current fighter policy was based on the Curtiss P-40 and Bell P-39 airplanes. New upcoming design plans were based on the Lockheed P-38 and Republic P-47.

The early XP-51 and R.A.F. Mustangs had a maximum speed of 387 miles per hour, which was higher than all other modern fighters of that period including the Spitfire and Messerschmitt Bf-109E. It clearly proved it was a better fighter than both the Curtiss P-40E and Bell P-39D in tests at Wright Field.

The Royal Air Force used the Mustang in service as an Army Co-operation aircraft. It first saw service at Dieppe, France in support of commando troops on July 27, 1942. It also saw service with the Royal Canadian Air Force as Mustang IA. Fitted with four 20 mm cannons, it became known as the "Train Buster" of Europe.

To the amazement of Army Air Force officials, the two XP-51's passed all flight tests at Wright Field successfully. The Air Force then ordered 460 P-51 fighters and 500 A-36 dive bomber aircraft. The A-36 was a P-51 aircraft which was fitted with wing dive brakes and could carry two 500 lb. bombs under the wings. They were used operationally in North Africa, Sicily, and in India.

In the fall of 1942, the Army Air Force attache in London, Major Tomas Hitchcock proposed that since the P-51 aircraft was the best fighter airframe to date that it should be married to a Rolls Royce "Merlin" engine. His idea and words were heard and four Mustangs were delivered to Rolls Royce for conversion. A four-bladed prop was fitted and a small "beard" type radiator was added in the nose. Tests were flown six weeks later and they were so successful that North America immediately ordered a redesign of the engine mount and airframe structure to handle the Merlin engine.

The Packard Company in the United States was brought in to handle the United States production of the Merlin engine to meet the production needs of this new Mustang aircraft. With this installation, the Mustang became the best high-altitude fighter in the world. It had everything—speed, altitude, and maneuverability.

The first two P-51 Merlin conversions were originally designated XP-78 but later they were changed to XP-51B. The P-51B Mustang was a new breed of fighter with the Merlin engine. The outward lines were similar, but the airframe was beefed up considerably to handle the increased power of the Merlin engine. The belly radiator was lengthened and deepened. The carburetor air intake was moved below the nose. A heavy wing was employed to enable the P-51B to handle two 1,000 lb. bombs or two long-range gas tanks. All up speed was now better than 440 miles per hour at 25,000 feet.

North America built two production lines to handle the increase in orders; the P-51B's were built in Los Angeles and P-51C's were built in Dallas, Texas. Both planes were identical. The first fighter group to be equipped with the P-51B's in England became operational in the winter of 1943.

They flew their first mission to Kiel, Germany, round trip distance of 1,000 miles on December 13, 1943. The full effect of this was not felt by the Luftwaffe until the following spring of 1944 when "the little friends", P-51B's and C's escorted B-17 and B-24 bombers on a 1,000 mile round trip to Berlin. Up until now, the Luftwaffe had the opportunity to attack at will the unescorted bomber formations; but now the tide of aerial combat had changed. The P-51's were now capable of meeting the Luftwaffe on an equal basis high over Germany.

To improve visibility, the British fitted a Malcolm hood to their Mustang fighters. In 1944, North America redesigned the fuselage of the Mustang and a beautiful streamline bubble canopy was fitted. This new version was designated P-51D and was powered by a Packard Merlin V-1650-7 engine of 1,450 horsepower. The P-51D was produced in greater numbers than any other model. 6,502 were built at the Los Angeles factory and 1,454 were built in Dallas, Texas.

Mustangs were the only Allied fighter with sufficient range to accompany heavy B-17 and B-24 bombers on shuttle missions to Russia and Italy. The P-51D's were also based in the Pacific at Iwo Jima to escort B-29's to Japan.

Of the 960 P-51, P-51A, and A-36 aircraft built, only four remain in the United States—two P-51's and two A-36's aircraft. One is still flying, an A-36, owned by a doctor in Florida. The other A-36 is stored. One P-51 is undergoing reconstruction by Wally Erickson of Minneapolis, Minnesota. The other aircraft, a P-51A model, is being rebuilt to be flyable by The Air Museum at Ontario, California under the leadership of Jerry Lentz, a Northrop engineer. When completed in 1968, it will be painted in the colors and markings of the English-based 67th Tactical Recon-group, U.S. 9th Air Force. It will carry the code letters "AX-G" painted on the side.

A P-51D fighter pilot of World War II flew a plane few civilians today could hope to match. The aircraft cost $75,000 originally and it cost the United States Government approximately $50,000 to train the pilot to fly it.

Fighter planes are wicked looking and beautiful, and the P-51 Mustang was no exception—beautiful to look at but deadly to the enemy. Fighter pilots developed physical feelings for them like a frontiersman develops for his pack horse. Sometimes they would pat their fighter plane like it was an affectionate member of the family or a close friend. When one faced death each day, the bond of kinship grew and grew between pilot and plane.

The great dame Merlin brought life to an otherwise cold, metallic airframe. The sound of the Merlin was clear and distinct; it was the heart of the Mustang. The red hydraulic fluid surged throughout the system much in the same manner as the life blood in a human. The top Aces flew the P-51 Mustang as if it were a part of them—anticipating their every need and maneuver. Some of the world's greatest aerial combats were made in the skies over Europe during 1943-1945 in Mustang fighters.

A photo-recon fighter was required by the Air Force, and so 91 P-51B's and P-51C's were modified into F-6C aircraft carrying Fairchild K-17 and K-24 cameras. A number of P-51D's were converted into F-6D's at the Dallas factory. Ten two-place TP-15D trainers were built with dual controls for the Army Air Force.

The Australian government built P-51D's under license, but the war ended before they could participate in the war against Japan.

The P-51 Mustang fighter served with the following air forces of Italy, France, Sweden, England, Australia, Canada, Philippines, Israel, South Korea, Nationalist China, Bolivia, Guatemala, Dominican Republic, Honduras, and Nicaragua.

The next production model was the P-51K built at the Dallas factory. It was identical to the P-51D model but was fitted with an Aero-Products four-bladed propeller. The photo-recon version of this aircraft was the F-6K.

The experimental department at Los Angeles designed the first in a series of light-weight fighters in the Mustang series. The first of these was the XP-51F. Fully loaded, it weighed just over 9,000 lbs. It carried only four, 50 caliber machine guns and had a three-bladed Aero-Products propeller. A saving of some 2,000 lbs. was made. A maximum speed of 465 miles per hour was attained by the XP-51F. Only three test models were built, and one was sent to the Royal Air Force for tests.

Two more light-weight Mustangs were built. The XP-51G was designed to use a new Rolls Royce Merlin 145 engine of 1,500 horsepower. It drove a five-bladed rotor propeller. Fully loaded, it was one of the lightest fighters built. It attained a speed of 470 miles per hour at 20,000 feet. No P-51E designation was assigned. The first production light-weight Mustang materialized with the P-51H model. Five hundred fifty-five were built. It had a Packard V-1650-9 Merlin and drove a four-bladed Aero-Products propeller. It had a maximum range of 1,500 miles with drop tanks fitted and had a maximum speed of 487 miles per hour at 25,000 feet.

After the war, the P-51H model was flown by several Air National Guard Squadrons. One is currently flying under civilian registration in the United States. It is owned by an airport operator in Ohio. Another P-51H model is being put together by Mike Couches of Hayward, California.

The final light-weight Mustang model was the XP-51J. Two of these were built and were similar to the XP-51F except they had an Allison V-1710-119 engine of 1,500 horsepower. The carburetor intake was fitted inside the belly radiator and a clean, smooth engine cowling encased the powerful engine. Unfortunately, none of these experimental light-weight Mustangs are preserved today.

The Mustang is still being flown by several Central and South American countries. A large number are registered on the United States Civil Register, and even a few are still being flown for pleasure in Canada, Australia, and New Zealand.

Designed during the stress of war, the P-51 Mustang fighter successes were phenomenal. High victory scores were run up by Air Force pilots and the P-51 Mustang made more pilots "Aces" than any other Allied fighter. It created many wartime records:

It was the first and only fighter to fly over all three enemy capitals—Rome, Tokyo, and Berlin.

It was the first fighter to escort bombers to Berlin and return.

It was the first fighter to fly the shuttle bomber missions to Russia, Italy, and North Africa.

As time will prove, the Mustang will emerge as one of the great, immortal fighters of World War II.

We wish to acknowledge the pictorial assistance of the following persons:
Tom Piedimonte
Jerold Lentz
Robert Brooks
North American Aviation
Colonel G. B. Jarrett
Ken Sumney
George Gasney
United States Air Force
Major Eugene Sommerich
Roger Besecker
Merle Olmsted
Frank Mormillo
William Larkins

North American P-51 has just been rolled out from factory and is ready for delivery to Wright Field.

The North American XP-51 at Langley Field, Virginia December 1941. While stationed at Langley, it underwent N.A.C.A. wing tests.

The original North American XP-51 for the United States Army. This 100-day miracle fighter was known as the "Apache" and was one of three delivered for tests.

This Mustang MK. I AG 348 was one of 20 supplied the Royal Air Force during World War II. It was used by both the Royal Air Force and the Royal Canadian Air Force Army Co-operation Command.

Royal Air Force Mustang MK-I AL-958 taken over by Army Air Force for tests. This model was fitted with the Allison V-1710-F3R engine of 1,000 horsepower.

Army Air Force P-51 flies over the Pacific Ocean on final acceptance test. Army took delivery of 150 of this model.

The United States P-51 "Apache" on cross-country flight over Texas. The first production model for the Army Air Force mounted four, 20 mm cannon. The maximum speed was 378 miles per hour.

First production order for the P-51 airplane mounted four 20 mm cannon. The P-51 was at first passed over by the Army, but later this opinion changed as tests compiled at Wright Field clearly showed that this fighter was superior to both the P-39 and P-40 fighter aircraft in speed and maneuverability.

This is the second model of two XP-51 B's which were converted Mustangs MK III's. It is shown here displaying an assortment of Royal Air Force tail stripes and fuselage code letters while wearing American insignia.

One of two XP-51B Mustangs built for the Air Force. They were originally designated XP-78. This was the first in the famous Mustang series that featured the proven Packard V-1650 "Merlin" engine. This XP-51 B mounted four, 20 mm cannon.

First production model of 400 P-51 B-1-NA Mustangs built for the Air Force. The reliable Merlin engine enabled this aircraft to fly better than 440 miles per hour and take on the best Luftwaffe Me-109's or Focke Wulf 190's over Europe.

North American P-51 B at an advance air strip in Burma 1943. Note 500-lb. bomb under wing These aircraft were used to pound the retreating Japanese army in Burma.

This North American P-51 C was modified in the field to carry cameras. It was redesignated F6C-10-NT upon its completion. This aircraft is shown here at an advanced air base in Burma 1944.

This North American P-51 C-10-NA had two Japanese fighter victories while operating in Burma 1944.

The latest wartime design in the Mustang series was the P-51 D model. It featured a new bubble canopy which gave increased pilot visibility. The aft fuselage was also lowered.

Two P-51 D Mustang fighters on a fighter sweep. They are from the 360th Fighter Squadron, 356th Fighter Group. Their black and yellow cowl markings were a distinct recognition feature.

Two P-51 D's from the famous 35th Fighter Group escort a 13th Air Force F5F Photo-recon "Lightning" on a photo-intelligence mission to Northern Luzon during the last days of the Philippine campaign.

Colorful line of Mustangs of the 3rd Air Commando's at their base on Luzon Island. The men of the 3rd Air Commando Wing were a cosmopolitan group of fighter pilots Most were veterans of other war theaters.

North American Aviation flight line at Los Angeles 1944. F-6 D photo-recon fighter is in foreground. Production P-51 D's in background await final repairs for check flight.

To hide their sleek Mustang aircraft from enemy eyes, pilots kept them under camouflage nets in revetments such as this to protect them as much as possible.

One of the large factors contributing to the Mustang's high speed was the way the Packard engine of the Mustang was neatly cowled. Panel lines are clearly shown. All panels were aluminum construction except one below the exhaust stacks which was made of stainless steel. Note the oil drain outlet pipe.

Uncowled Packard V-1650-7 engine of the Mustang coolant tank is mounted in front. Carburetor air intake is on bottom. Big supercharger is mounted in rear.

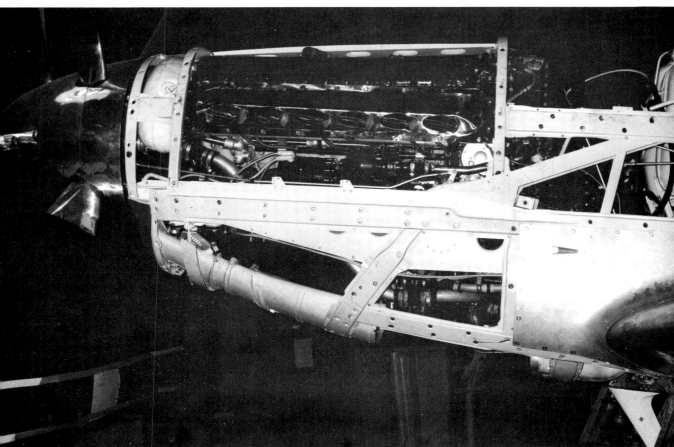

Unusual view of North American P-51 A. This aircraft was on display at The Air Museum in Ontario, California. It is now undergoing restoration for flying purposes. Its first flight is scheduled for spring 1968.

Landing gear close-up detail on P-51 D Mustang. Gear and doors were hydraulically activated. Arc 3 radio antenna mast is mounted in front of doors. Engine air scoop is at lower rear.

ROYAL AIR FORCE Mustang I

North American P-51B Mustang of the 354th Fighter
Group. This was one of the first U.S. fighter groups to
be equipped with the Mustang.

NORTH AMERICAN P-51B "Mustang"

Royal Air Force Mustang I. This model was thoroughly
tested by the R.A.F. and found superior to the Curtiss
P-40 Kittyhawk.

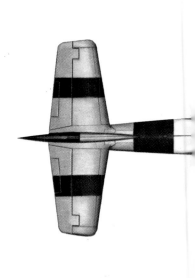

U.S. ARMY AIR FORCE P-51D-25-Na

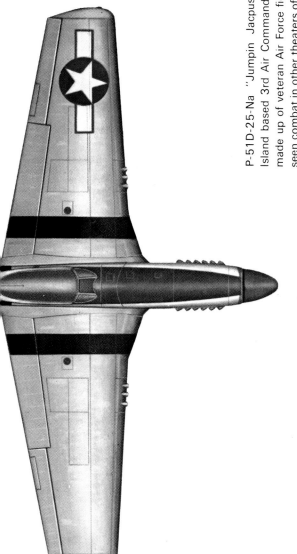

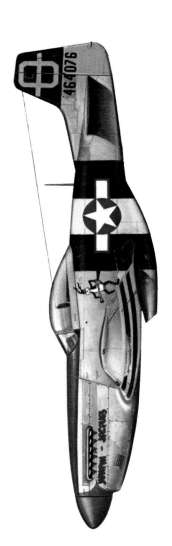

P-51D-25-Na "Jumpin Jacpus" of the Philippine Island based 3rd Air Commandoes. This group was made up of veteran Air Force fighter pilots who had seen combat in other theaters of war.

Uwe Feist

Scale: 1:72

U.S. ARMY AIR FORCE P-51B-15-Na

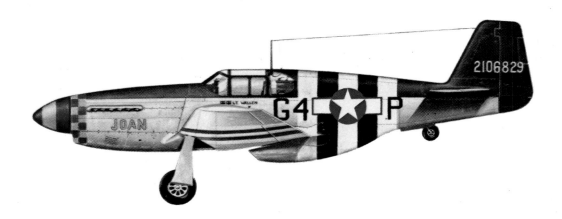

U.S. Army Air Force P-51B-15-Na flown by Lt. Wallen of the 357th Fighter Group and named after his girl. Note invasion stripe markings.

P-51D "Mustang"

P-51D Mustang "Lou IV." One of the most colorful Mustangs to come out of the World War II period.

U.S. ARMY P-51D-30-NA
AIR FORCE SER. NO. 44-69080

CREW WEIGHT 200 LBS.

C\C
P. MORGAN
D. FRALEY

Fighter pilots during the war kept visual scoreboard records on their aircraft by painting their aerial victories on the fuselage side. Some pilots put them on canopy frame. Note landing light in wheel well.

Major Walker Muhurin stands beside his favorite aircraft in the Philippines. His P-51 D was named "The Chief."

Instrument panel of North American P-51 D-30-NT. Flight instruments are grouped on the left and engine instruments are grouped on right.

Close up of panel below instrument panel shows the fuel shut-off lever, external fuel tank release, ignition switch, primer, starter, and super-charger switch.

Left side cockpit console of Mustang. Flare-gun holder is just below arm rest. Rudder and aileron trim nose are at lower center. Landing gear lever is at lower front with the throttle control at top front. Two bomb salvo knobs are just below.

Right side of cockpit of Mustang was well planned and laid out for pilot convenience. Electrical switches and circuit breakers are at lower front with the Arc 3 radio-push-button control at lower rear.

With the introduction of the bubble canopy on the P-51 D series pilot's visibility increased 360 degrees. Note clean low-drag wing to fuselage fillet lines.

A 500-lb. bomb is shackled under wing of Army Air Force A-36 A in North Africa for targets on the Italian-held island of Pantalerra. Note wing dive brake under wing.

This colorful P-51 D-30-NT bears black and white invasion stripes. A World War II D-Day recognition feature of all Allied planes used to ease visual identification.

P-51 D at the Ontario Air Museum. The name "Spam Can" was a term coined by Pacific fighter pilots during World War II.

A Dallas-built F-6K Photo-recon Mustang rests proudly on the ramp. During the war, Dallas-built Mustangs were easily identifiable by the slight bulge on the aft part of the canopy. Los Angeles division bubble canopies were straight.

Royal Australian Air Force P-51K-15-Nt Mustang. Note post war insignia and how it differs from other R.A.A.F. Mustangs illustrated.

F-51D Mustang high over Korea returns to base after close support mission over enemy lines.

P-51D Mustang flies over a Southern California area after making a successful test hop.

With two 110-gallon long-range, fuel tanks, this United States Air Force Mustang could fly across the United States non-stop.

A formidable weapon in any air force, the Mustang still serves as a first-line fighter in several Central and South American countries. This P-51D is on a fighter training flight. Note the Zero-length rocket launcher racks.

F-51 D from Lowry Air Force Base Training Command. Mustang flies high over a Colorado valley with the Rocky Mountains in the background.

Captain George Lake of the California Air National Guard guns the Merlin engine on this short field take off.

U.S. Army Air Force F-6D photo-recon Mustang at the North American factory at Los Angeles, California.

This F-51 D "Ceece" named after the famous television cartoon character was used by N.A.C.A. at Edwards Air Force Base. Note the tall rudder on the P-51 D and insignia on nose.

Philippine Air Force P-51 D at its home base at Nichols Field, Luzon. The Mustang was used operationally until 1959 when they were replaced by F-86F Saberjets.

The F-51 D was used by the Philippine Air Force until late 1959. The Mustang above is shown at Clark Field.

First of two North American XP-51 G light-weight Mustangs which used a British Rolls Royce 145 Merlin engine driving a five-bladed Rotol propeller. It had a maximum speed of 472 miles per hour.

Profile of clean North American XP-51 J. This light-weight fighter model employed an Allison V-1710-119 of 1,500 horsepower. Only two were built.

Remarkable North American XP-51 F was one of three built in early 1944 as first lightweight Mustang.

The North American P-51 H became the light-weight Mustang production aircraft and is seen here flying off the Santa Barbara coast.

The P-51 H could carry six, five inch high velocity air rockets and two 500 lb. bombs in addition to six 50 caliber M.G. A number were sent to the Pacific for combat against the Japanese; however the Pacific War ended before their real qualities could be shown.

A P-51 H "High in the Sky." The P-51 H was designed and built to have a service life of only 500 hours. All aircraft were then supposed to be scrapped. The United States Air Force found that the P-51 H model could well go beyond 500 hours, and many were flown several thousand hours without any difficulties.

Profile of the P-51 H-5-NA shows the deep fuselage lines of the aircraft. The plane was slab-sided to house a longer coolant radiator. Note that the tail-wheel gear doors have been removed and tail wheel fixed in the down position.

P-51 H-5-NA in Air Force Marking. This was one of 555 built at the Los Angeles division of North American.

This Royal Australian Air Force Mustang A 68-105 has been preserved in Moorabbin Air Museum. It saw service with the Royal Australian Air Force after World War II.

A P-51D in Bolivian Air Force markings FAB 511. Bolivia took delivery of four Mustangs in 1966. Note the United States registration number.

This Bolivian Air Force TP-51 D FAB-510 is getting its final check flight before long hop to South America.

A civilian-owned Australian Mustang MK XXI registered VH-PLB at Moonshine, Australia. A relatively few Mustangs are still flying down under.

In 1949, Jimmie Stewart sponsored a converted North American F-6 C Mustang piloted by Joe de Bona. It took first place in the Bendix Trophy Race. He averaged 470 miles per hour from Los Angeles to Cleveland.

Following the end of armed hostilities, the Bendix Air Race was begun again in 1946. This 1946 Bendix Race entry was flown by a previous Bendix Race winner, the famous woman pilot Jacqueline Cochran.

Paul Mantz's 1948 Bendix Racer was a bright fire engine red color with white trim. It may be seen at Movieland of the Air Museum, Santa Ana, California.

In 1948, Paul Mantz flew this P-51 C to victory in the Bendix Trophy Race. Scoreboard on fuselage side shows that he received over $125,000 in total winnings.

One of the fastest and most famous racing Mustangs of all time was this P-51 D "Galloping Ghost."
It always placed in the money during the last four Thompson Trophy Races. It is now owned by Doctor
Cliff Cummins and is flown regularly as a pleasure aircraft.

Mustang race entry of Jimmie Stewart bore the nickname "Thunderbird." The entire wing was sealed
up and used as a gas tank permitting long-range, non-stop flights. This aircraft was later sold and was
lost on delivery flight due to pilot error.

Bob Hoover taxis his P-51 D Mustang past the reviewing stand after his demonstration flight at the Las Vegas Air Races.

Mr. Alex. a converted military Mustang. was seen at several post-war air shows. This model of Mustang has become almost extinct.

There are approximately fifty P-51 D Mustangs on the United States civil register.

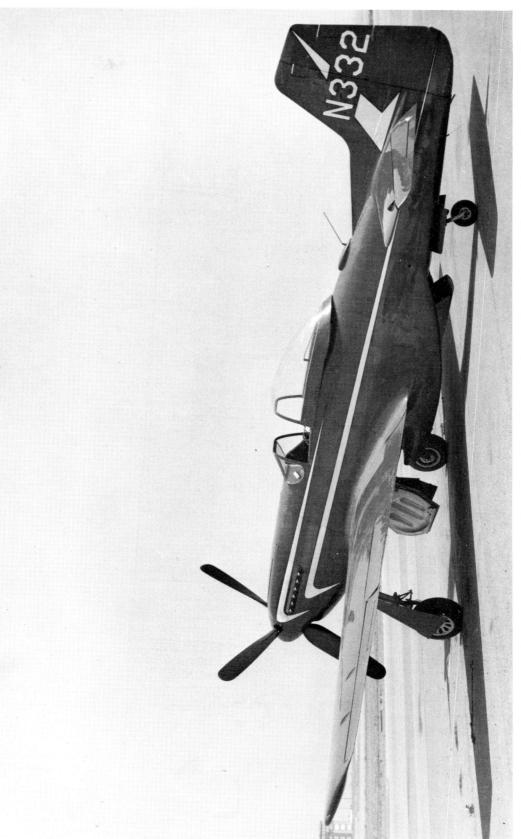

This P-51 D Mustang won the 1964 Clearwater, Florida to Reno, Nevada, cross-country air race. It was flown by Wayne Adams and sponsored by Maytag.

Civilian owned A-36 A racer No. 2 at the 1949 Cleveland Air Races. This aircraft was a stock aircraft and was flown in both the Tinnerman and Thompson Air Races.

P-51 A in special test camouflage of blue and white at Wright Field. North American P-51A on factory test hop. Its speed amazed Air Force officials.

P-51C-10-Na Mustang of the National Chinese Air Force. Aircraft was painted a flat olive drab with a gray bottom.

"Warrior At Rest." This P-51B painted in invasion markings belongs to the 362nd Fighter Group, United States 9th Air Force.

A P-51D-5-Na with special red trim and markings. Pilot of this Mustang fighter named it "Chip."

P-51C and P-51D of the French Air Force during occupation duty at Neubiberg, Germany. Note "Cross of Lorraine" squadron insignia on tail.

This P-51D was one purchased by the Swedish Air Force from U.S. Army Air Force and was later sold to Israeli Air Force for use during the Sinai War 1956.

The Luftwaffe also flew the P-51D Mustang. Several good examples were captured intact and were used to trail Allied bomber formations giving speed, direction, and bomber's altitude to attacking German fighters.

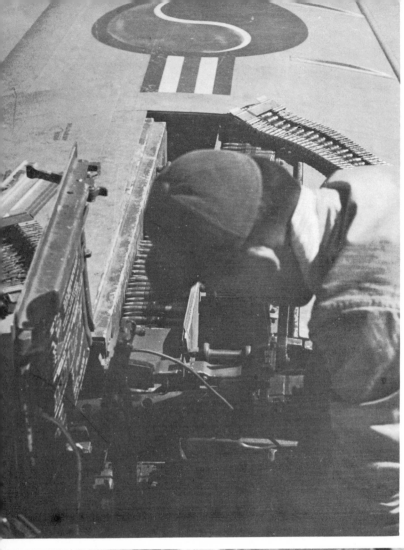

South Korean Air Force mechanic feeds 50 caliber ammunition into one of Mustang's six 50 caliber machine guns.

R.O.K. fighter pilot awaits take-off orders for mission over North Korea. Note K-17 gunsight behind windscreen.

In-flight view of R.O.K. unit of P-51 D's led by Colonel Dean Hess, commander of the 6146th Air Base Squadron.

Line up of South Korean Air Force P-51 D Mustangs. This unit was led by Lieutenant-Colonel Dean Hess who flew the second P-51 D number 18. He later had the name "Last Chance" painted on the side cockpit.

P-51D Mustang Serial No. 44-63528 with a pair of Marquardt ram jet engines.

	NUMBER BUILT	ENGINE	MAXIMUM SPEED	RANGE	CEILING	SPAN	GROSS WEIGHT	LENGTH	ARMAMENT
P-51A	460	Allison V-1710-81	387 mph at 20,000'	450 miles	31,000'	37'0"	8,000 lbs.	32'3"	(4) 50 cal. MG = P-51A (4) 20 mm cannon = P-51
A-36A	500	Allison V-1710-87	360 mph at 20,000'	550 miles	30,000'	37'0"	8,370 lbs.	32'3"	(6) 50 cal. MG (2) 500 lb. bombs
P-51B/C	3,750	Packard V-1650-3	440 mph at 25,000'	900 miles	42,000'	37'0"	9,800 lbs.	32'3"	(4) 50 cal. MG (2) 1,000 lb. bombs
P-51D	8,252	Packard V-1650-7	437 mph at 25,000'	1,000 miles	42,000'	37'0"	10,100 lbs.	32'3"	(6) 50 cal. MG (2) 1,000 lb. bombs
XP-51F	3	Packard V-1650-7	465 mph at 30,000'	650 miles	42,500'	37'0"	7,600 lbs.	32'3"	(4) 50 cal. MG
XP-51G	2	Merlin 145 1,500 h.p.	470 mph at 20,000'	500 miles	45,700'	37'0"	7,260 lbs.	32'3"	(4) 50 cal. MG
P-51H	555	Packard V-1650-9	487 mph at 25,000'	850 miles	42,000'	37'0"	9,500 lbs.	33'4"	(6) 50 cal. MG (2) 500 lb. bombs
XP-51J	2	Allison V-1710-119 1,500 h.p.	490 mph at 25,000'	650 miles	44,000'	37'0"	7,550 lbs.	32'11"	(4) 50 cal. MG
P-51K	1,337	Packard V-1650-7	430 mph at 25,000'	1,000 miles	40,000'	37'0"	10,000 lbs.	32'3"	(6) 50 cal. MG
TP-51D	10	Packard V-1650-7	435 mph at 25,000'	600 miles	38,000'	37'0"	11,300 lbs.	32'3"	(6) 50 cal. MG

"Mustangs for Korea"—This overhaul line was set up to modify P-51 D's for use in Korea. The Mustang was again called up for service during the Korean War.

Fifty-odd F-51 D Mustangs line the ramp at Nellis Air Force Base, Nevada at the annual Nellis gunnery meet.

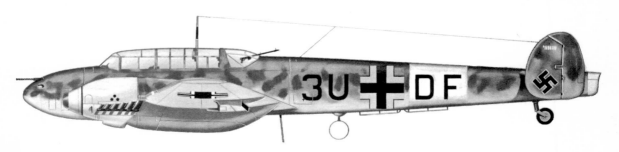
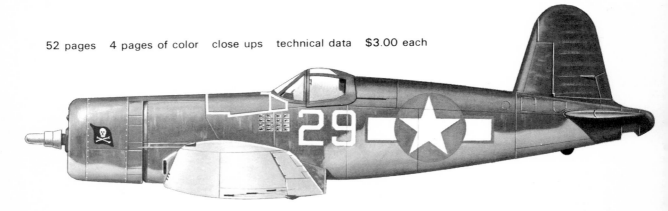